Improve your sight-reading!

A piece a week

Grade 2

Paul Harris

FABER *ff* MUSIC

Thanks to Jean Cockburn, Diana Jackson, Karen Marshall, Naomi Marshall, Ann Priestley and Flora Tzanetaki for help and inspiration!

Music setting by Jackie Leigh
Cover and page design by Susan Clarke
Printed in England by Caligraving Ltd

ISBN10: 0-571-53938-6
EAN13: 978-0-571-53938-3

To buy Faber Music publications or to find out about the full range of titles available
please contact your local music retailer or Faber Music sales enquiries:
Faber Music Ltd, Burnt Mill, Elizabeth Way, Harlow CM20 2HX
Tel: +44 (0) 1279 82 89 82   Fax: 44 (0) 1279 82 89 83
sales@fabermusic.com   fabermusicstore.com

Contents

Introduction

Why?

One of the main reasons why so many young pianists can't sight-read is simply because they don't spend enough time actually looking at and processing notation. It's not uncommon to spend many weeks (perhaps even longer) learning just one or two pieces. The pieces are really learnt by ear and tactile memory – the notation becomes more of an aide-memoire, symbols that nudge kinaesthetic memory.

So we need to encourage pupils to spend more time literally looking at notation! That's the purpose of this book. It's a one-a-week or, at most, one-every-two weeks collection of pieces that will be especially useful when a pupil is moving towards a grade exam.

Not actually sight-reading

These pieces are not to be sight-read: the idea is to learn one piece each week so that pupils are constantly having to process new notation in a comfortable time frame. They will have to actually LOOK at new music more often and so will become less nervous and more able to deal with it. It will begin to take the fear and panic out of reading notation.

Standard

Each piece is significantly easier than an equivalent grade piece. Each is built on a different (and interesting) pianistic idea, sits comfortably under the hands and has lots of repetition.

Practice

It's important that pupils practise these pieces regularly – every day, ideally – so that they are regularly reading notation. A new piece each week for 26 weeks before an exam will make a huge difference.

Ingredients

Each piece is based on a small number of ideas – simple rhythms and note patterns – but have quite a number of dynamics and other markings: these are very important. Pupils very rarely manage to include dynamics and other markings in exams. This takes practice and these pieces will give them that opportunity!

Fingering

There is a certain amount of fingering marked. It's very important that pupils learn that the point of fingering is simply to get your hand to the right place so that the notes can be played. Once that point is understood it all becomes so much more achievable. It's very important that this connection is made.

Pulse

It's interesting that many pupils really don't understand the importance of pulse. By playing new pieces regularly and thinking about the pulse each time, there is much more chance that the concept will be understood and then applied successfully to actual sight-reading! Insist that pupils always think and set the pulse before they begin playing.

It's essential that the pulse set is manageable. If it's too fast and the pulse is constantly unstable, the concept will take much longer to fully digest.

Paul Harris

Indian chief

6

Watercolours

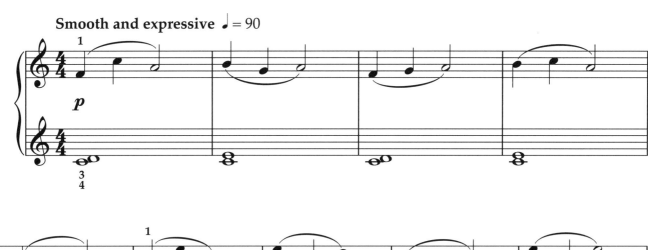

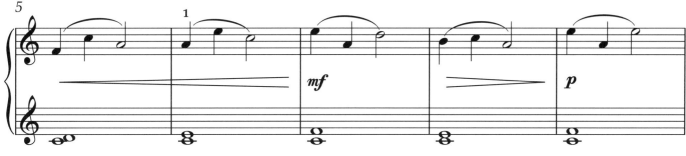

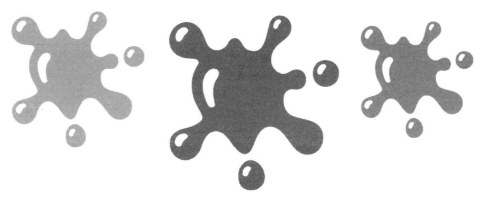

Skipping and hopping

Machines

With energy ♩ = 120

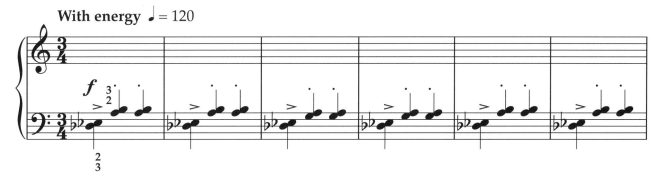

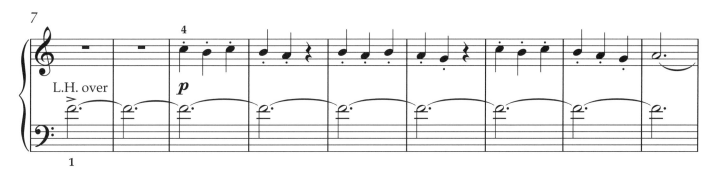

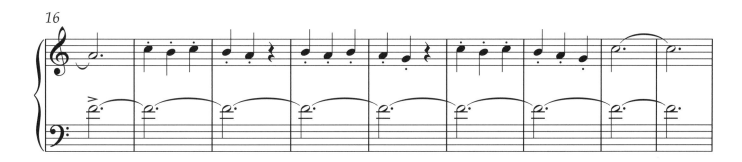

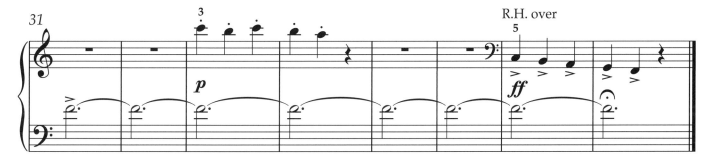

Day dreaming

Three-legged race

Keep really steady! ♩ = 100

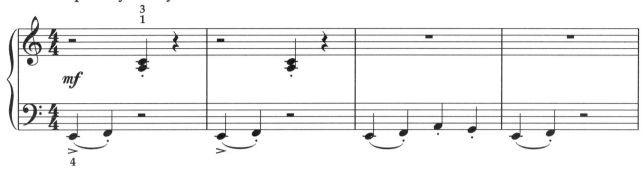

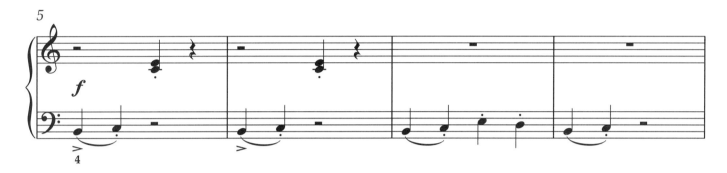

Pebble skimming

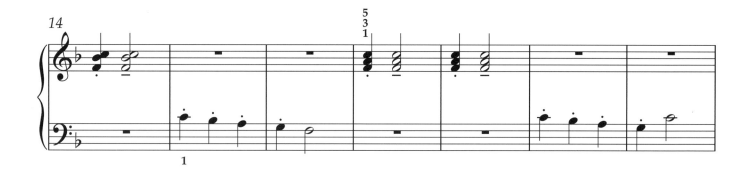

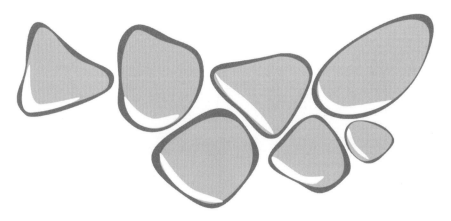

Spooks ✓

Halloween!

Quite fast (but spooky) ♩ = 110

*Hold these notes down
silently throughout*

13

Dancing round the maypole

Spies on a mission

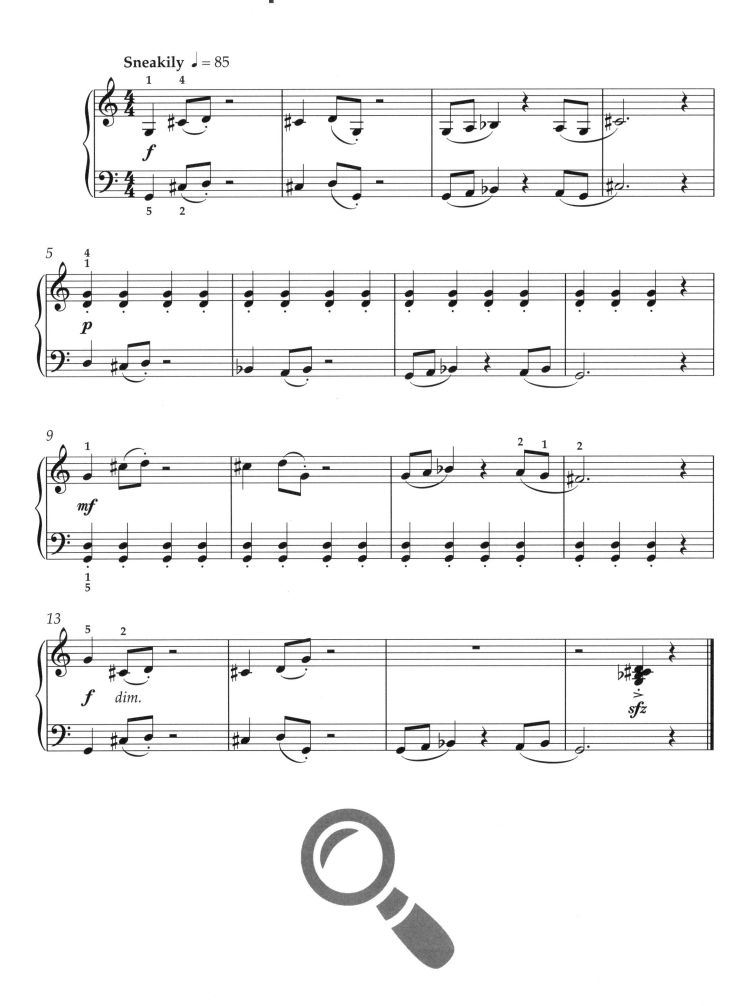

Rushing around

Lonely

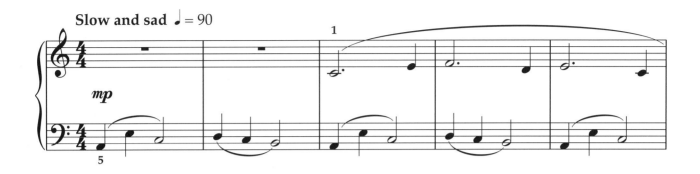

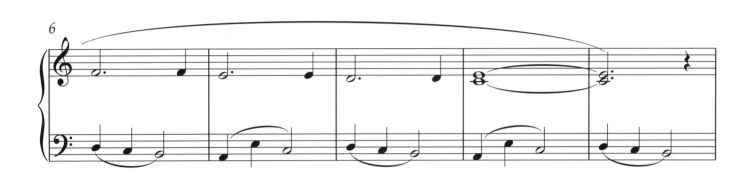

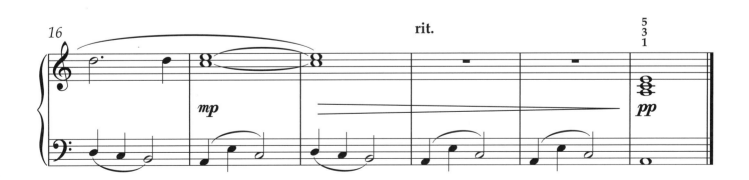

China Town

Quick and light ♩ = 140

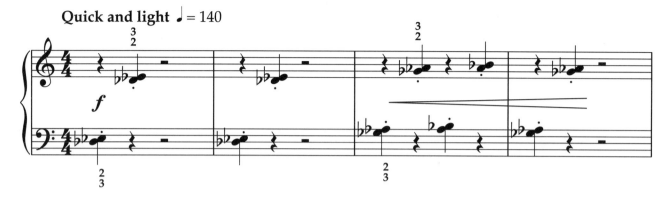

Lost

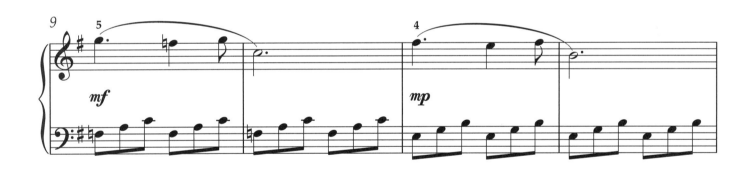

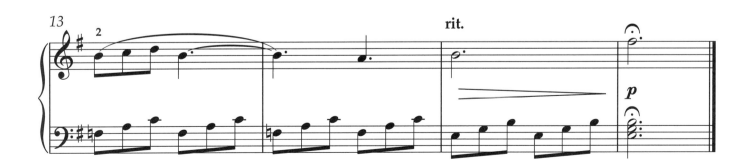

Traffic jam

Danger ahead!

March tempo ♩ = 105

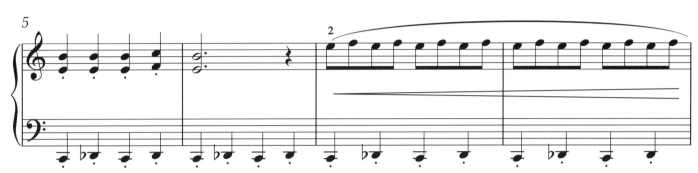

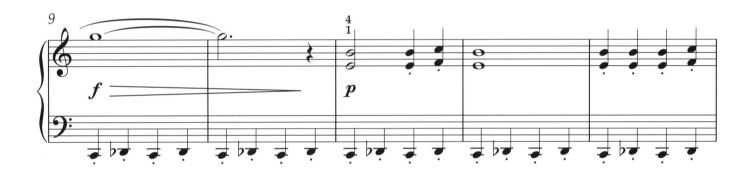

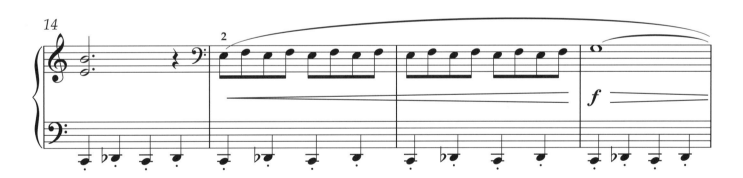

pause until the sound disappears

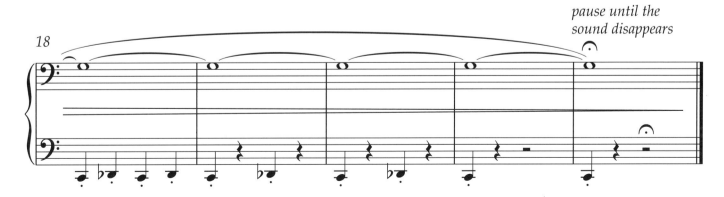

Elephants take a stroll

Busy people

23

Kites in the sky

Rolling hills

Don't be put off by the flats!

The magical mirror

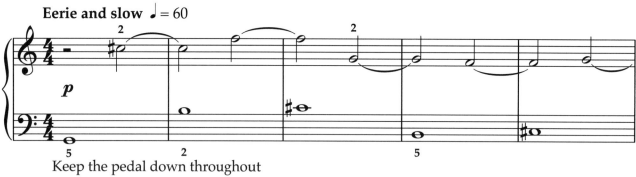

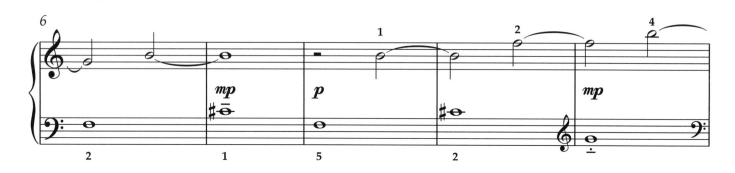

Keep the pedal down throughout

Catch me if you can!

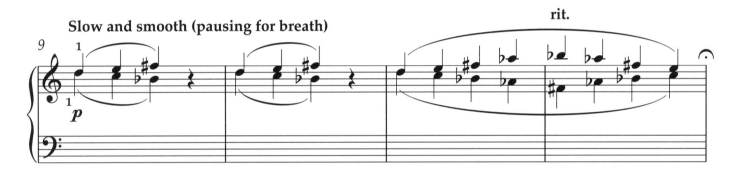

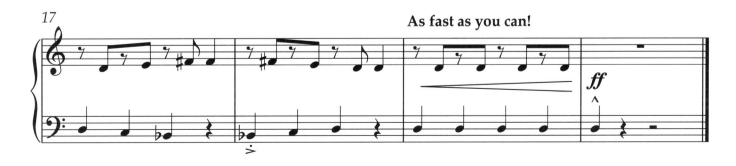

Butterflies

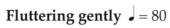

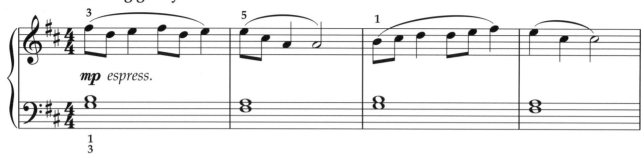

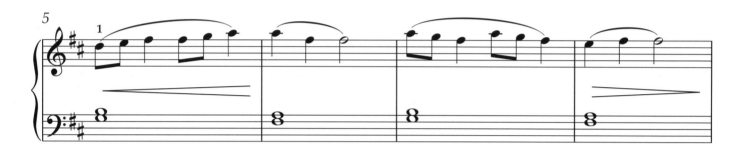

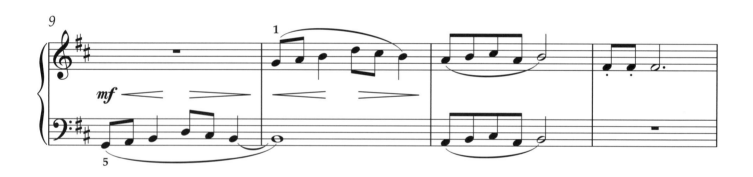

Waterfall

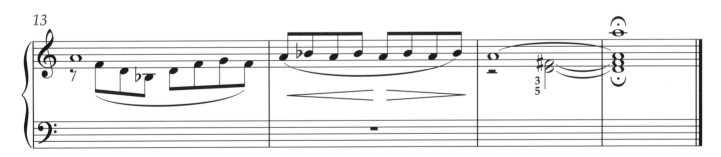

29

In the clouds

Slow ♩. = 50

pp sempre

Hold the keys down for the duration of the bar
Hold the sustaining pedal down throughout if possible

Secret agent TX9 saves the world

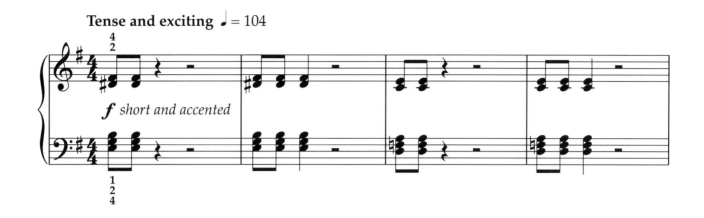

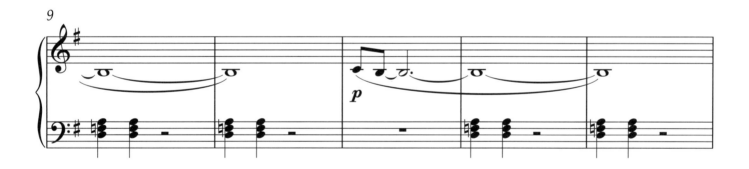

Activities page

This wordsearch and questions are based on musical elements
you'll find in all the pieces in this book.

F	O	R	T	I	S	S	I	M	O	N	N	M
V	C	W	G	I	Y	S	D	A	I	R	T	X
C	H	F	I	B	R	P	T	E	Y	U	A	W
K	O	N	H	C	R	E	S	C	E	N	D	O
W	R	B	Z	Y	P	T	L	P	C	L	P	E
O	D	N	E	U	N	I	M	I	D	U	A	N
Z	S	V	M	V	S	I	R	B	N	E	U	M
E	S	P	R	E	S	S	I	V	O	M	S	L
J	H	S	T	N	E	C	C	A	O	Q	E	A
Z	X	N	M	F	E	L	C	S	S	A	B	D
S	V	I	G	M	N	L	H	L	G	B	Y	E
Y	Y	M	E	Z	Z	O	P	I	A	N	O	P
Q	S	L	U	R	S	T	A	C	C	A	T	O

PAUSE

CRESCENDO

ACCENTS

TRIADS

STACCATO

MEZZOPIANO

DIMINUENDO

ESPRESSIVO

FORTISSIMO

SLURS

RIT

BASS CLEF

PEDAL

CHORDS

Match a piece to each of these clues

Has the dynamic *pp* sempre: _____

Every left-hand note has an accent: _____

Every left-hand note is *staccato*: _____

A piece with F major triads: _____

Has a *diminuendo* hairpin that lasts for six bars: _____

Has the word *espressivo* in its shortened form: _____

Has a *sforzando* in the final bar: _____

Contains two-bar slurs: _____

Is *piano* all the way through: _____

Has a *rit.* that lasts for three bars: _____

The right hand uses the bass clef: _____